T0130452

Grandma Bonnie's Cats
In Love Again

Bonnie Tweedy
- Illustrations by Dan Cooper -

© 2011 Bonnie Tweedy. All rights reserved.

No part of this book may be reproduced, stored in a retrieval system, or
transmitted by any means without the written permission of the author.

AuthorHouse™
1663 Liberty Drive
Bloomington, IN 47403
www.authorhouse.com
Phone: 833-262-8899

Because of the dynamic nature of the Internet, any web addresses or links contained in this book may have changed
since publication and may no longer be valid. The views expressed in this work are solely those of the author and do not
necessarily reflect the views of the publisher, and the publisher hereby disclaims any responsibility for them.

Any people depicted in stock imagery provided by Getty Images are models,
and such images are being used for illustrative purposes only.
Certain stock imagery © Getty Images.

This book is printed on acid-free paper.

ISBN: 978-1-4520-1150-9 (sc)
ISBN: 978-1-4817-2211-7 (e)

Library of Congress Control Number: 2010917143

Print information available on the last page.

Published by AuthorHouse

Rev. Date: 11/15/2021

authorHOUSE®

Dedication

To my granddaughter Randi
who gave me the sweetest kitten ever.

Grandma Bonnie was starting to feel happy again. The sad time was over and now it was time to love the cats that were lucky enough to stay in Grandma Bonnie's back yard.

Mama stayed because she was not easy to catch and after all she was the mother of all the baby kittens. She loved each one as much as Grandma Bonnie did.

There was Baby and Grey Feather of course. They were the first born and Grandma Bonnie had a special bond with them. Baby had been so helpful to Grandma Bonnie when the Newspaper and TV people had come to take pictures and Grandma Bonnie was thankful for her help.

Jetta stayed too. He was the wise old owl who helped Grandma Bonnie take care of the other cats. Jetta talked with his eyes and Grandma Bonnie always knew what he was telling her.

Pip was the indoor cat. Grandma Bonnie chose her because Pip would sleep with Grandma Bonnie every night. Grandma Bonnie would miss her too much if she wasn't there. Sometimes Pip would sit with Grandma Bonnie on her chair and they would watch TV together.

Grandma Bonnie's Granddaughter Randi and her three boys Peter, David and Leo came over to visit Grandma Bonnie quite often. The boys liked to play with all the cats. Peter, David and Leo were Grandma Bonnie's Great Grandchildren.

One day there was a knock on the door. It was Randi, Grandma Bonnie's Granddaughter and her three boys. Randi said "I have a surprise for you, Grandma Bonnie.

Boy did she ever have a surprise. Oh! Oh! Grandma Bonnie cried. It was a little Kitten only four weeks old. Randi had found him behind her door. He was lost from his mother. He was sooooo cute.

Grandma Bonnie named the new Kitten Buffy because he was Buff and Black with a little Black face and blue eyes. Grandma Bonnie had to get up in the night to bottle feed Buffy milk because he was so little and not able to eat food.

By this time, PaPa Roy wasn't feeling very well and he often laid down on the couch in the living room. Buffy liked PaPa Roy. They would cuddle up together on the couch and lie there all afternoon.

Grandma Bonnie loved Buffy and Buffy loved Grandma Bonnie. Grandma Bonnie was in love once again.

Printed in the United States
by Baker & Taylor Publisher Services